50 GREAT

Tiffin Recipes

50 GREAT

Tiffin Recipes

Master Chefs of India

Lustre Press
Roli Books

We are grateful to Arun Ganapathy,
GJV Prasad, Kalp Mithal, Prima Kurien,
Vijaylakshmi Baig, Bina Parasramka,
and Jeani Mohindra for their contribution.

ISBN: 81-7436-370-X

© Roli & Janssen BV 2005
Published in India by Roli Books
in arrangement with Roli & Janssen
M-75 Greater Kailash II (Market)
New Delhi 110 048, India
Ph: ++91 (11) 29212271, 29212782
Fax: ++91 (11) 29217185
E-mail: roli@vsnl.com, Website: rolibooks.com

Editor: Neeta Datta, *Design:* Sneha Pamneja,
Layout design: Kumar Raman, *Production:* Naresh Nigam

Printed and bound in Singapore

Introduction

Awide variety of delectable snacks occupy an important space in Indian cuisine, so much so that there is even a special word to describe them: *tiffin*. The word, derived from tiffing, an old English dialect or a slang word, means to take a little drink or sip. It only makes sense, then, that from this derivative, the word tiffin has been transformed into the equivalent of taking small bites from various dishes.

The light lunch or snack, packed in metal tiffin boxes, is now a ubiquitous phenomenon in India. In Bombay, tiffin delivery has been perfected to an art. Lunches prepared for working-men by their wives are forwarded to them by *dabbawallas* who use a complex system to get thousands of tiffin-boxes to their destinations on a daily basis. Tiffin carriers come in different shapes and sizes, the most common one being the steel carrier comprising small bowls stacked one upon the other so that dry and liquid foods do not mix.

In South India, tiffin refers to a mid afternoon snack, that is to be had at three in the afternoon, followed by a cup of piping hot South Indian coffee. Delicious *idli, dosa,* and *uppuma* are some of the (many) choices to snack upon. Many South Indian dishes, such as the ones mentioned above, use rice as the base ingredient to make for a satisfying snack. In North India, the variety is no less. There is a delicious variety of dishes made with dal, cottage cheese, and potato. From kebabs to pakoras, these snacks are as good as a light meal that will stimulate your palate.

50 Great Tiffin Recipes gives you the best of vegetarian snacks from North and South India—a veritable treat of afternoon delights.

Basic Preparations

Buttermilk (*chaas*)

Take 2 cups / 400 gm yoghurt (*dahi*), whisked; a pinch of asafoetida (*hing*); salt to taste; 1 green chilli, finely chopped; 1" piece ginger (*adrak*), finely chopped; a few curry leaves (*kari patta*); 1 tbsp / 4 gm green coriander (*hara dhaniya*), finely chopped; and 4 cups / 1 lt water.

Mix the yoghurt with the other ingredients (except water). Add water and mix well. It makes an excellent drink in summer.

Coconut Milk

Grate 1 coconut and press through a muslin cloth to obtain the first (thick) extract. Boil the grated coconut with equal quantity of water to obtain the second (thin) extract.

Note: *If refrigerated, this can stay for up to 3-4 days.*

Gun Powder

Take 100 gm split black gram (*urad dal*); 50 gm dry red chillies (*sookhi lal mirch*); 2 tsp / 5 gm mustard seeds (*rai*); 1 tsp asafoetida (*hing*); 20 gm curry leaves (*kari patta*); 1 tsp lime concentrate; and salt to taste.

1. In a wok (*kadhai*), dry roast the split black gram on low heat for 5-8 minutes. Keep aside. Dry roast the dry red chillies and mustard seeds, separately.
2. Add all the ingredients together and grind to a fine powder. Store in an airtight jar. Serve with ghee.

Imli Ki Chutney (Tamarind chutney)

Take 100 gm tamarind (*imli*); 200 gm jaggery (*gur*); 1½ tsp / 6 gm black salt (*kala namak*); 2 tsp / 8 gm salt; 1½ tsp / 3 gm cumin (*jeera*) seeds, roasted, powdered; 4-5 green cardamom (*choti elaichi*), powdered; ½ tsp ginger powder (*sonth*).

1. Soak the tamarind and jaggery together for 4-5 hours.
2. Mash the two thoroughly with a wooden spoon or rub between your palms. Strain through a muslin cloth.
3. Add the remaining ingredients and bring the mixture to the boil, stirring continuously.
4. Cool and preserve.

Note: *If refrigerated, this can stay for about 15-20 days.*

Sambhar Powder

Take 75 gm dry red chillies (*sookhi lal mirch*); ½ tbsp / 15 ml vegetable oil; 200 gm coriander (*dhaniya*) seeds; 50 gm cumin (*jeera*) seeds; 20 gm fenugreek seeds (*methi dana*); 20 gm black peppercorns (*sabut kali mirch*); 20 gm mustard seeds (*rai*), 20 gm Bengal gram (*chana dal*); 20 gm red gram (*arhar dal*); 20 gm poppy seeds (*khus khus*); 2 cinnamon (*dalchini*) sticks; 5 curry leaves (*kari patta*), and 20 gm turmeric (*haldi*) powder.

1. Fry the dry red chillies in oil. Dry roast all the other ingredients (except turmeric powder) separately till they release a strong aroma.
2. Grind all the ingredients including turmeric powder together to a fine powder. Store the powder in an airtight container and use when required.

Cottage Cheese (*paneer*)

For about 400 gm of cottage cheese; boil 2 lt of milk in a deep pot and remove from heat. Add 160 ml vinegar or lemon juice till the milk curdles. Transfer the curdled milk into a muslin cloth to drain out the whey. Use either in crumbled form or else wrap in a muslin cloth and press down with a weight for half an hour or so. This will form into a block, which can then be cut to desired size pieces.

Tamarind (*imli*) Juice

The juice extracted by soaking a lemon-sized tamarind in 2 cups of hot water for 20 minutes. Wash the tamarind in this and rinse and drain the water for the extract.

Tomato Chutney

Take 2 kg tomatoes, washed, quartered; 1 cup / 200 ml vegetable oil; 1 kg onions, peeled, quartered; 15 dry red chillies (*sookhi lal mirch*); 2 tsp mustard seeds (*rai*); 20 gm split black gram (*urad dal*); 10 sprigs curry leaves (*kari patta*); and salt to taste.

1. Heat a little oil in a wok (*kadhai*); add the onions and fry for 8-10 minutes till translucent. Add the dry red chillies and tomatoes. Cook for 15-20 minutes. Remove from heat. When the mixture cools, grind to a fine paste.
2. Heat 1 tbsp oil in the same wok; add the mustard seeds, split black gram, and curry leaves. Sauté for a few minutes. Add this to the paste and check for seasoning. Serve cold.

South Indian
Tiffin Recipes

Ulundu Vada

Deep-fried black gram rounds

INGREDIENTS:

Split black gram (urad dal)	1 cup / 150 gm
Salt	2 tsp / 8 gm
Asafoetida (hing)	a pinch
Ginger (adrak), 1" piece	1
Green chillies	3
Dry red chillies (sookhi lal mirch)	2
Vegetable oil for deep-frying	

Serves: **4**

METHOD:

1. Soak the split black gram for 2 hours. Drain and grind with the remaining ingredients (except oil) to a smooth batter. Divide the batter equally and

shape into rounds (traditionally these are circular with a small hole in the middle) on a banana leaf or on your palm.

2. Heat the oil in a wok (*kadhai*); carefully lower the rounds, in small batches, and deep-fry till crisp and golden brown. Remove and drain the excess oil on absorbent kitchen towels.

3. Serve hot with *sambhar* (see p. 50) and coconut chutney (see p. 51).

Amavadai

Deep-fried mixed gram rounds

INGREDIENTS:

Bengal gram (*chana dal*),
soaked for 1 hour ⅔ cups / 100 gm
Black gram (*urad dal*),
soaked for 1 hour 1 cup / 150 gm
Red gram (*arhar dal*),
soaked for 1 hour ⅔ cup / 100 gm
Dry red chillies (*sookhi lal mirch*) 2
Salt to taste
Asafoetida (*hing*) a pinch
Vegetable oil 2½ cups / 500 ml

Serves: **6**

METHOD:

1. Drain the grams and grind with dry red chillies, salt, and asafoetida to a coarse batter.

2. Heat the oil in a pan. Roll the gram mixture into

balls and flatten on the palm into thick, small rounds (or on a piece of banana leaf, keeping the leaf on your left palm, flatten out the paste with the tips of finger).

3. Deep-fry the rounds in the hot oil till golden brown on both sides. Remove and drain the excess oil on absorbent kitchen towels. Repeat till all the rounds are fried.

4. Serve hot with coconut chutney (see p. 51).

Sabu Dana Vada

Sago patties—South Indian style

INGREDIENTS:

Sago (*sabu dana*)	½ cup / 100 gm
Buttermilk (*chaas*), (see p. 6)	½ cup / 100 ml
Gram flour (*besan*)	½ cup / 50 gm
Red chilli powder	1 tsp / 2 gm
Asafoetida (*hing*)	a pinch
Green chillies, chopped	2
Green coriander (*hara dhaniya*), chopped	1 tbsp / 4 gm
Ghee	1 tsp / 5 gm
Salt to taste	
Vegetable oil for frying	

METHOD:

1. Soak the sago in buttermilk for 30 minutes.
2. Add all the ingredients (except oil) to the soaked sago. Pour enough water to make a stiff batter.
3. Divide the sago batter into equal portions and shape each portion into round patties.
4. Heat the oil in a wok (*kadhai*); add a few patties at a time and deep-fry for 15-20 minutes or till golden brown. Remove with a slotted spoon, and drain the excess oil on absorbent kitchen towels.
5. Serve hot with coconut chutney (see p. 51).

Serves: 4

Thair Vada

Black gram dumplings in spiced yoghurt

METHOD:

1. Grind the black gram to a paste. Add the next six ingredients. Beat into a stiff batter; keep aside.
2. Crush the cumin seeds, mustard seeds, and dry red chillies coarsely and fry the mixture in oil with the curry leaves and green chillies.
3. Beat the yoghurt with this spice mixture, salt, and 1 cup water. Keep aside.
4. Gently fry spoonfuls of the black gram batter in hot oil until golden. Remove and drain. Transfer the dumplings into a pot of water for just a few seconds. Remove, gently squeeze out the excess water and add to the spiced yoghurt.
5. Serve chilled.

INGREDIENTS:

Black gram (urad dal), soaked overnight, drained	500 gm
Salt to taste	
Lemon (nimbu) juice	1 tbsp / 15 ml
Asafoetida (hing), soaked in ½ cup water	½ tsp / 2½ gm
Ginger (adrak), crushed	1 tbsp
Green chillies, finely chopped	2
Curry leaves (kari patta), chopped	½ cup / 7½ gm
Cumin (jeera) seeds	1 tsp / 2 gm
Mustard seeds (rai)	½ tsp / 1½ gm
Dry red chillies (sookhi lal mirch)	2
Vegetable oil	2 tsp / 10 ml
Curry leaves, chopped	½ cup
Green chillies	4
Yoghurt (dahi)	2½-3½ cups
Salt to taste	

Serves: 6

17

Adai

Rice and mixed gram pancakes

INGREDIENTS:

Rice	2 cups / 400 gm
Split red gram (*arhar dal*)	1 cup / 160 gm
Split Bengal gram (*chana dal*)	½ cup / 80 gm
Split black gram (*urad dal*)	½ cup / 75 gm
Dry red chillies (*sookhi lal mirch*)	4-5
Salt	3 tsp / 12 gm
Asafoetida (*hing*)	2-3 pinches
Vegetable oil for frying	

Serves: **6**

METHOD:

1. Soak the rice and the grams for 2 hours. Drain and grind with dry red chillies, salt, asafoetida and some water to make a thick batter.

2. Heat a griddle (*tawa*) and smear 1 tsp oil over it. Spread a ladleful of the batter from centre outwards in circular motions with the ladle itself.

3. Fry till one side is golden brown. Then flip and fry till the other side is crisp and golden brown.

Remove and repeat till all the batter is used up.

4. Serve hot with jaggery or a blob of butter.

Masala Dosa

Black gram pancakes with potato stuffing

INGREDIENTS:

Rice, soaked for 4 hours	¾ cup / 150 gm
Split black gram (*urad dal*), soaked for 4 hours	¼ cup
Salt to taste	

For the filling:

Vegetable oil	2 tbsp / 30 ml
Onion, large, sliced	1
Mustard seeds (*rai*)	1 tsp / 3 gm
Split green gram (*moong dal*)	1 tbsp / 18 gm
Bengal gram	1 tbsp / 25 gm
Dry red chillies (*sookhi lal mirch*)	2
Cashew nuts (*kaju*)	4 tsp / 20 gm
Curry leaves (*kari patta*)	a few
Potatoes, boiled, mashed	2
Turmeric (*haldi*) powder	1 tsp / 2 gm

Serves: **4-6**

METHOD:

1. Drain and grind the rice and split black gram together. Add salt and a little water to make a smooth batter.
2. **For the filling,** heat the oil

and sauté the onion till translucent. Add mustard seeds, split green gram, and Bengal gram; sauté for 3-4 minutes. Add the remaining ingredients and cook for 3-4 minutes more.

3. Pour a ladleful of the batter on a griddle and spread it evenly.

Sprinkle a little oil around the sides and cook till golden brown. Put 2 tbsp filling in the centre of the pancake and fold as desired. Remove and repeat till all the batter and filling are used up.

4. Serve hot with *sambhar* and coconut chutney (see p. 50 & 51).

Rava Dosa

Semolina pancakes

INGREDIENTS:

Semolina (*suji*)	1½ cups / 150 gm
Refined flour (*maida*)	1 tbsp / 10 gm
Rice flour	2 cups / 200 gm
Yoghurt (*dahi*)	¼ cup / 50 gm
Asafoetida (*hing*)	a pinch
Curry leaves (*kari patta*)	4-5
Salt to taste	
Mustard seeds (*rai*)	¼ tsp
Cumin (*jeera*) seeds	½ tsp / 1 gm
Green chillies, chopped	3-4
Ginger (*adrak*), chopped	a small piece
Vegetable oil for frying	

METHOD:

1. Mix the semolina, refined flour, rice flour, yoghurt, asafoetida, curry leaves, and salt together. Add water to make a thin batter.

2. Heat ½ tsp of oil; add the mustard seeds, cumin seeds, and green chillies. When the seeds start spluttering, remove and pour into the batter. Mix in the ginger.

3. Heat the griddle (*tawa*) and smear some oil. Pour a ladleful of batter and tilt the griddle from side to side so that the batter spreads evenly. When the edges turn up, flip the pancake to cook the other side as well. Repeat till all the batter is used up.

4. Serve hot.

Serves: **4**

Achaar Idli

Steamed pickled cakes

METHOD:

1. Drain the split black gram and grind to a fine paste by adding a little water.
2. Drain the semolina and grind with the fenugreek seeds.
3. Mix the two pastes and add enough water to make a batter of dropping consistency. Season with salt.
4. Take the *idli* moulds. Pour 1 tbsp of the batter in each mould, put some mixed pickle over it and then top with another tbsp of the batter.
5. Steam for 20 minutes.
6. Serve hot with gun powder (see p. 7) and coconut chutney (see p. 51).

INGREDIENTS:

Split black gram (*urad dal*), soaked
for 2 hours   2½ cups / 375 gm
Semolina (*suji*), soaked for
20 minutes   2 cups / 200 gm
Fenugreek seeds (*methi dana*)   1 tsp / 3 gm
Mixed pickle, chopped   ¼ cup / 50 gm
Salt to taste

Serves: **8 - 1 0**

Idli

Fluffy rice cakes

INGREDIENTS:

Parboiled rice	2¼ cups / 450 gm
Black gram (*urad dal*)	1 cup / 150 gm
Salt to taste	

Serves: **8-10**

METHOD:

1. Soak the rice and black gram separately (in enough water to cover) for about 4 hours or keep overnight and grind separately. Grind the rice

into a coarse batter and the black gram into a smooth batter. Mix the two batters together. Add salt. Set aside for 8-10 hours to ferment in a big vessel as the batter will rise as it ferments.

2. Boil the water in an *idli* steamer. Smear the moulds with a little oil.

3. Drop a ladleful of the *idli* batter in the moulds and steam for 15 minutes. Allow it to cool and remove. Repeat till all the batter is used up.

4. Serve with *sambhar* (see p. 50) and coconut chutney (see p. 51).

Sevain Idli

Steamed vermicelli cakes

INGREDIENTS:

Split black gram (*urad dal*),
   soaked for 2 hours   I cup / 150 gm

Semolina (*suji*), soaked
   for 20 minutes   I cup / 100 gm

Fenugreek seeds
   (*methi dana*)   I tsp / 3 gm

Vermicelli (*sevain*), soaked
   for 20 minutes   2 cups

Salt to taste

METHOD:

1. Drain the split black gram and grind to a fine paste by adding a little water.
2. Drain the semolina and grind with the fenugreek seeds.
3. Mix the two pastes together; add the drained vermicelli and season with salt.
4. Take the idli *moulds*; pour 1 tbsp of the batter in each mould and steam for 20 minutes. Allow it to cool and remove. Repeat till all the batter is used up.
5. Serve hot with coconut chutney (see p. 51).

Serves: **8-10**

26

Arvi Bonda

Crispy colocasia

INGREDIENTS:

Colocasia (*arvi*), boiled, mashed	500 gm
Green chillies, chopped	6
Yoghurt (*dahi*)	1 tbsp / 30 gm
Ginger (*adrak*), chopped	1 tsp / 6 gm
Asafoetida (*hing*)	a pinch
Green coriander (*hara dhaniya*), chopped	1 tbsp / 4 gm
Salt to taste	

For the batter:

Refined flour (*maida*)	1 cup / 100 gm
Gram flour (*besan*)	½ cup / 50 gm
Rice flour	½ cup / 50 gm
Bicarbonate of soda	a pinch
Vegetable oil for frying	

METHOD:

1. Mix the colocasia with green chillies, yoghurt, ginger, asafoetida, and green coriander. Season with salt and shape the mixture into medium-sized balls.

2. Combine all the ingredients of the batter (except oil) and add enough water to make a batter of semi-thick consistency.

3. Heat the oil in a wok (*kadhai*); dip the colocasia balls into the batter and then deep-fry, in small batches, on medium heat until crisp. Remove and drain on absorbent kitchen towels.

4. Serve hot.

Serves: **4**

Urulaikizhangu Bonda

Potato fritters

METHOD:

1. Heat the oil in a wok (*kadhai*); sauté both the seeds, black gram, and curry leaves till the gram turns golden brown. Add onions, green coriander, green chillies, and chilli powder; fry for a minute.
2. Add the potatoes, salt, and lemon juice; mix well. Remove and keep aside to cool. Then mash until the mixture is smooth. Divide and shape the mixture into egg-sized balls.
3. **For the batter**, mix all the ingredients till it is coating consistency.
4. Coat the balls in the batter and fry them in the oil till light brown. Remove and drain the excess oil.
5. Serve hot with coconut chutney (see p. 51).

INGREDIENTS:

Potatoes, boiled, peeled, cut into small pieces	I kg
Vegetable oil	I tbsp / 15 ml
Mustard seeds (*rai*)	2 tsp / 6 gm
Cumin (*jeera*) seeds	2 tsp / 4 gm
Black gram (*urad dal*), washed	6 tsp
Curry leaves (*kari patta*)	4 cups / 100 gm
Onions, thickly diced	2
Green coriander (*hara dhaniya*), finely chopped	8 cups / 200 gm
Green chillies, finely chopped	4
Red chilli powder	I tsp / 2 gm
Salt to taste	
Lemon (*nimbu*) juice	6 tsp / 30 ml
Vegetable oil for deep-frying	
For the batter:	
Gram flour (*besan*)	1½ cups / 150 gm
Bicarbonate of soda	a pinch
Salt	I tsp / 4 gm

Serves: **8-10**

29

Urundai Kozhakatai

Steamed savoury dumplings

INGREDIENTS:

Rice, broken	2½ cups / 500 gm
Vegetable oil	1 tbsp / 15 ml
Mustard seeds (*rai*)	½ tsp / 1½ gm
Dry red chilli (*sookhi lal mirch*)	1
Bengal gram (*chana dal*)	2 tbsp / 50 gm
Asafoetida (*hing*)	a pinch
Salt to taste	
Coconut (*nariyal*), grated	3 tbsp / 12 gm

Serves: **6**

METHOD:

1. Heat the oil in a pan; sauté the mustard seeds until it starts crackling. Add dry red chilli and sauté for a while. Add

Bengal gram and sauté till the gram turns golden brown.

2. Add rice, asafoetida, salt, and just enough water to cover the rice. Cook for 10 minutes. Add coconut and mix well. Remove from heat and keep aside to cool.

3. Divide the mixture equally into small balls and steam for 15 minutes in a steamer. Repeat till all the mixture is used up.

4. Serve hot.

Bajji

Vegetable fritters

INGREDIENTS:

Vegetables of choice (potatoes,
   onions, aubergines, and
   plantains), thinly sliced
Vegetable oil for frying

For the batter:

Gram flour (*besan*)	I cup / 100 gm
Rice flour	½ cup / 50 gm
Red chilli powder	½ tsp / I gm
Salt to taste	
Asafoetida (*hing*)	a pinch
Yoghurt (*dahi*)	I tbsp / 30 gm

METHOD:

1. **For the batter,** mix all the ingredients together adding very little water to make a thick batter.
2. Heat the oil in a wok (*kadhai*); dip each vegetable slice in the batter and deep-fry till golden. Remove with a slotted spoon and drain the excess oil on absorbent kitchen towels.
3. Serve hot.

Serves: **4**

To prevent raw bananas and
aubergines from turning black
after slicing, drop them in a bowl
of water mixed with a little
yoghurt.

Achappam

Crunchy savouries

INGREDIENTS:

Rice flour	5 cups / 500 gm
Coconut (nariyal), grated	2 cups / 200 gm
Eggs, whisked till stiff	2
Sugar	3 tbsp / 60 gm
Sesame (til) seeds	2 tsp / 6 gm
Salt to taste	

Serves: **6-8**

METHOD:

1. Extract 2¾ cups milk from the grated coconut (see p. 6).
2. Mix the rice flour with coconut milk into a smooth batter. Add the eggs; mix well. Add sugar, sesame seeds, and salt. Use less sugar or the batter will stick to the mould.
3. Heat some oil in a wok (*kadhai*). When hot, place the *achappam* mould into the oil for 10 minutes or until the mould becomes hot. Lift the mould carefully, dip into the batter, then place it back into the oil. When the *achappam* turns light brown, gently shake the mould to remove it. Leave in the oil for another 2 minutes until golden. Lift and drain. Repeat the process till all the batter has been used.
4. Cool and store in airtight jars.

Line an airtight tin with blotting
paper to store fried foodstuff for
a longer time.

Vengaya Pakoda

Onion fritters

INGREDIENTS:

Onions, peeled, chopped	3
Vegetable oil for deep-frying	

For the batter:

Gram flour (*besan*)	1 cup / 100 gm
Rice flour	½ cup / 50 gm
Red chilli powder	½ tsp / 1 gm
Salt to taste	
Asafoetida (*hing*)	a pinch
Ghee	2 tsp / 10 gm

METHOD:

1. **For the batter,** mix all the ingredients together, adding very little water to make a thick batter. Mix the onions into the batter.
2. Heat the oil in a wok (*kadhai*); carefully lower small amounts of the onion batter mix into the hot oil and deep-fry till golden. Remove and drain the excess oil on absorbent kitchen towels. Repeat till all the batter is used up.
3. Serve hot.

Serves: **4**

Aval Uppuma

Beaten rice cooked with potatoes

METHOD:

1. Heat the oil in a pan; sauté the mustard seeds until it starts crackling. Add the potatoes, turmeric powder, green chillies, and salt. Sprinkle some water and cook till the potatoes are tender.
2. Add the beaten rice, mix well and cook for a few minutes till all the water is absorbed and the mixture is dry. Remove from heat. Wait for the mixture to cool a bit and then add lemon juice.
3. Serve garnished with green coriander.

Variation: *Use yoghurt instead of potato and turmeric powder to make yoghurt with beaten rice.*

INGREDIENTS:

Beaten rice (*chidwa*), thick variety, soaked in warm water for 7 minutes, drained	2 cups / 100 gm
Vegetable oil	2 tbsp / 15 ml
Mustard seeds (*rai*)	½ tsp / 1½ gm
Potatoes, medium-sized, cut into small cubes	2
Turmeric (*haldi*) powder	¼ tsp
Green chillies, chopped	2
Salt to taste	
Lemon (*nimbu*) juice	1 big or 2 small
Green coriander (*hara dhaniya*), chopped	a small bunch

Serves: **4-6**

Rava Uppuma

Tempered semolina with vegetables

INGREDIENTS:

Semolina (*suji*)	I cup / 100 gm
Vegetable oil	3 tsp / 15 ml
Ghee	2 tsp / 10 gm
Mustard seeds (*rai*)	½ tsp / 1½ gm
Split black gram (*urad dal*)	½ tsp
Cashew nuts (*kaju*)	8
Ginger (*adrak*), 1" piece, finely chopped	1
Asafoetida (*hing*)	a pinch
Green chillies, roughly chopped	2-3
Curry leaves (*kari patta*)	4-5
Salt to taste	
Green coriander (*hara dhaniya*), chopped	a small bunch

Serves: **4**

METHOD:

1. Dry roast the semolina in a pan till light golden.
2. Heat the oil and ghee; add the mustard seeds, split black gram, cashew nuts, ginger, asafoetida,

green chillies, and curry leaves; sauté.

3. Pour 2 cups of water into the pan. Add salt and bring the mixture to the boil.

4. Add the semolina, stirring constantly so that it does not form lumps. Remove when all the water is absorbed and the mixture is cooked.

5. Garnish with green coriander and serve with coconut chutney (see p. 51).

Variation: *You can add any vegetable of your choice.*

Bread Uppuma

Bread cooked with onion
and tomatoes

INGREDIENTS:

Bread	10-12 slices
Vegetable oil	2 tsp / 10 ml
Mustard seeds (*rai*)	¼ tsp
Cumin (*jeera*) seeds	½ tsp / 1 gm
Onions, peeled, chopped	2
Tomatoes, chopped	2
Green chillies, chopped	2
Turmeric (*haldi*) powder	¼ tsp
Red chilli powder to taste	
Salt to taste	

Serves: **4**

METHOD:

1. If it is refrigerated old
   bread and slightly hard,
   soak it in water for 30
   seconds.
2. Break the bread into small
   pieces.

3. Heat the oil in a pan; sauté the mustard seeds and cumin seeds till the seeds start spluttering. Add the onions and cook till it changes colour. Add the tomatoes, green chillies, turmeric powder, red chilli powder, and salt.

4. Cook for 2 minutes. Add the bread and stir for a further 2-3 minutes. Remove and serve hot.

Etheka Appam

Banana fritters

INGREDIENTS:

Bananas, ripe, chopped lengthwise into 4 pieces	500 gm
Rice flour	½ cup / 50 gm
Sugar	1 tsp / 3 gm
Baking powder	½ tsp / 3 gm
Water	½ cup / 125 ml
Vegetable oil for frying	

METHOD:

1. Mix the rice flour, sugar, baking powder, and water together into a smooth batter.
2. Heat the oil in a wok (*kadhai*); dip the banana in the batter and deep-fry, one at a time, till golden brown. Remove with a slotted spoon and drain the excess oil on absorbent paper towels. Repeat till all the bananas are fried.
3. Serve hot.

Serves: **8**

A few drops of lemon juice added
to cut bananas or apples prevents
them from turning black.

Masala Uttapam

Spicy rice and black gram pancakes

INGREDIENTS:

Rice	¾ cup / 150 gm
Split black gram (*urad dal*)	¾ cup / 112 gm
Salt to taste	
For the filling:	
Vegetable oil	¼ cup / 50 ml
Onion, large, finely chopped	1
Tomatoes, large, finely chopped	2
Green chillies, finely chopped	4
Cumin (*jeera*) seeds	1 tsp / 2 gm
Green coriander (*hara dhaniya*), finely chopped	2 tbsp / 8 gm
Salt to taste	

METHOD:

1. Prepare the batter by grinding together rice, split black gram, a little water, and salt. Keep aside.
2. **For the filling,** heat a little oil in a pan; add all the ingredients and mix well. Cook for a few minutes. Remove and keep aside.
3. Heat a non-stick pan; pour a ladleful of the batter and spread it evenly. Cook on medium heat.
4. Spread the filling over the batter, sprinkle a little oil around the sides and cook until the pancake is brown on the underside. Turn and cook the other side as well. Remove and repeat till all the batter is used up.
5. Serve hot with coconut chutney (see p. 51).

Serves: **5-6**

Godumai

Wheat flour pancakes

INGREDIENTS:

Wholewheat flour (*atta*)	2 cups / 200 gm
Rice flour	1 cup / 100 gm
Buttermilk (*chaas*), (see p. 6)	½ cup / 100 ml
Salt to taste	
Green chillies, finely chopped	2

For the tempering:

Vegetable oil	½ tbsp / 8 ml
Mustard seeds (*rai*)	¼ tsp
Cumin (*jeera*) seeds	½ tsp / 1 gm
Curry leaves (*kari patta*)	a few
Green coriander (*hara dhaniya*), chopped	1 tbsp / 4 gm

Serves: **4-6**

METHOD:

1. In a large bowl, mix wholewheat and rice flours with the buttermilk, salt, and green chillies. Add enough water to the mixture to make a batter of dropping consistency. Let it ferment for 1 hour.

2. **For the tempering,** heat the oil in a pan; add mustard seeds, cumin seeds, and curry leaves. Fry till the seeds start spluttering. Add the green coriander. Pour this tempering into the batter.

3. Heat a non-stick pan. Pour a ladleful of the batter and spread it evenly to make paper-thin pancake. Sprinkle a little oil around the sides and cook until golden brown.

4. Serve hot with coconut chutney (see p.).

Murruku

Rice coils

INGREDIENTS:

Gram flour (*besan*)	3 cups / 300 gm
Rice flour	1½ cups / 150 gm
Ghee	1 tsp / 5 gm
Cumin (*jeera*) seeds, broiled, powdered	½ tsp / 1 gm
Red chilli powder	½ tsp / 1 gm
Asafoetida (*hing*)	¼ tsp / 1 gm
Sesame (*til*) seeds	1 tsp / 3 gm
Vegetable oil for frying	

METHOD:

1. Mix the gram flour and rice flour together. Rub in the ghee with the fingertips till well incorporated. Add all the ingredients and mix well. Sprinkle some water and knead lightly.
2. Put some dough into the *murruku* mould and press out the *murruku*; deep-fry till golden brown. Remove and drain the excess oil on absorbent paper towels. Repeat until all the dough is used up.
3. Cool and store in airtight jars.

Serves: **6-8**

Spilt oil or ghee is easily cleaned up by spreading newspapers over it. These absorb the liquid and a wet rag can finish up the cleaning.

Basic Sambhar

Vegetables in red gram

INGREDIENTS:

Tamarind (*imli*), lemon-sized	1
Vegetables (drumsticks or / and potatoes, aubergines, etc), chopped	2
Asafoetida (*hing*)	a pinch
Curry leaves (*kari patta*)	5-6
Sambhar powder (see p. 8)	1½ tsp / 3 gm
Salt to taste	1½ tsp / 6 gm
Split red gram (*arhar dal*), cooked	½ cup / 80 gm
Rice powder	1 tsp
Vegetable oil	1 tsp / 5 ml
Dry red chillies (*sookhi lal mirch*)	2
Mustard seeds (*rai*)	¼ tsp
Fenugreek seeds (*methi dana*)	¼ tsp

Serves: **4**

METHOD:

1. Soak the tamarind in 1 cup of warm water for 5-10 minutes and squeeze out the juice.
2. Cook the vegetables with the tamarind juice. Add asafoetida, curry leaves, and enough water to cover the vegetables.
3. Add *sambhar* powder and salt; mix well.
4. When the vegetables are tender add the cooked split red gram and let it come to the boil.
5. If the mixture looks a little thin, add rice powder dissolved in a few spoons of water and boil for a minute. Remove.
6. Heat the oil in a pan; add dry red chillies, mustard and fenugreek seeds. Sauté till the seeds start spluttering. Remove and add to the *sambhar*.

Coconut Chutney

METHOD

1. Grind the coconut, ginger, 2 onions, 1 sprig of curry leaves, and 1 dry red chilli together into a smooth paste.
2. Heat 1 tsp oil in a pan; add the mustard seeds, the remaining dry red chillies, curry leaves, and onions; sauté for a while. Then add coconut paste and stir for a minute.
3. Add tamarind paste, mix well and remove from heat.
4. Serve as an accompaniment.

INGREDIENTS

Coconut (*nariyal*), grated	1 cup / 100 gm
Ginger (*adrak*), chopped	1¼ tbsp / 30 gm
Onions, finely chopped	4
Curry leaves (*kari patta*)	2 sprigs
Dry red chillies (*sookhi lal mirch*), large	3
Mustard seeds (*rai*)	½ tsp / 1½ gm
Tamarind (*imli*) paste	¾ tsp

Serves: **4-6**

North Indian
Tiffin Recipes

Moong Dal Ke Chille

Green gram pancakes

INGREDIENTS:

Split green gram (*dhuli moong dal*),
   soaked for 2 hours   1¼ cups / 250 gm

Ginger (*adrak*), finely chopped, 1" piece   1

Green chillies, finely chopped   2-3

Green coriander (*hara dhaniya*),
   finely chopped   4 tbsp / 16 gm

Red chilli powder   ½ tsp / 1 gm

Cumin (*jeera*) seeds   1 tsp / 1½ gm

Salt to taste

Vegetable oil for shallow frying

METHOD:

1. Drain the green gram and grind to a smooth paste.
2. Add the remaining ingredients except the oil and whip with a ladle for 2-3 minutes to make a semi-thick batter.
3. Heat a griddle (*tawa*); spread 3 tbsp of the batter to make a thin pancake. Add a little oil around the sides. When the underside is done, turn over with the help of a spatula and cook the other side till golden brown. Remove and repeat till all the batter is used up.
4. Serve hot with *hare dhaniye ki chutney* (see p. 94).

Serves: **4-5**

The green gram batter can be
refrigerated for a few days but
the pancakes should be made just
before serving.

Patrel

Colocasia leaf rolls

INGREDIENTS:

Colocasia leaves (*arvi ke patte*), centre stems removed	30
For the filling:	
Dry red / Green chillies (*sookhi lal / hari mirch*)	6
Ginger (*adrak*), 1" piece	1
Garlic (*lasan*)	1 pod
Cumin (*jeera*) seeds, roasted	1 tsp / 2 gm
Coriander (*dhaniya*) seeds, roasted	1 tsp / 2 gm
Cloves (*laung*)	6
Cinnamon (*dalchini*), 1" stick	1
Turmeric (*haldi*) powder	½ tsp / 1 gm
Bananas (*kela*), mashed	2
Green coriander (*hara dhaniya*), chopped	2 tbsp / 8 gm
Tamarind (*imli*) water	1 cup / 200 ml
Jaggery (*gur*)	2 tbsp / 40 gm
Salt to taste	
Vegetable oil	6 tbsp / 90 ml

Serves: **6-8**

METHOD:

1. **For the filling,** grind all the ingredients together (except oil) to make a thick paste, adding a little water if required.

2. Place an inverted colocasia leaf flat, spread the paste thinly over it, place another leaf on top and apply the paste again. Continue this process for 4-5 leaves if they are large or 8-10 leaves if they are small. Tuck in the sides and roll tightly, secure with a string. Similarly, make more such rolls.

3. Heat the oil in a pan; fry the rolls on all sides, then cover the pan with a lid containing some water. Reduce heat, stirring occasionally, and cook for 45 minutes to 1 hour. Remove.

4. To serve, cut the rolls into slices and shallow fry. Serve with lemon wedges.

Patrel if refrigerated can
stay for a week or so.

Chane Ke Kebab

Bengal gram kebabs

INGREDIENTS:

Bengal gram (*chana dal*)	2 cups / 300 gm
Salt to taste	
Coriander (*dhaniya*) powder	1 tsp / 1½ gm
Cumin (*jeera*) powder	½ tsp / ¾ gm
Green chilli paste	3 tbsp / 45 gm
Onion paste	4 tbsp / 100 gm
Garlic (*lasan*) paste	5 tsp / 30 gm
Yoghurt (*dahi*)	½ cup / 100 gm
Vegetable oil	2 tbsp / 30 ml
Water	2 cups / 500 ml
Roasted gram (*chana*), powdered	5 tsp / 25 gm
Garam masala	a large pinch
Sugar, powdered	½ tsp / 1½ gm
Vegetable oil for deep-frying	

METHOD:

1. Mix the Bengal gram with all the ingredients except roasted gram powder, garam masala, sugar, and oil. Boil till tender and dry.
2. Grind the mixture to a thick paste without using any water. Mix in the remaining ingredients and knead till the dough is soft and smooth.
3. Divide the dough into lemon-sized portions. Shape each portion into round patties.
4. Heat the oil in a wok (*kadhai*); deep-fry the patties on low heat till golden brown.
5. Serve hot with mint chutney (see p. 95).

Serves: 4

Makuni Litty

Baked bread stuffed with chick pea flour

METHOD:

1. Knead the wholewheat flour with water till soft. Divide the dough to make 5 cm balls.

2. In a bowl, mix the roasted chick pea flour, mustard oil, salt, and red chilli powder together. Keep the filling aside.

3. Take a portion of the dough, make a deep depression with your thumb and add 2 tsp of the filling. Pinch the edges to seal. Repeat with the other portions.

4. Bake the stuffed balls on charcoal embers turning them constantly so that they are uniformly baked and a light coloured crust is formed.

5. Serve hot with ghee, thick dal, and vegetables.

INGREDIENTS:

Wholewheat flour (*atta*)	3 cups / 300 gm
Roasted chick pea flour (*sattu*)	1 cup / 100 gm
Mustard (*sarson*) oil	2 tsp / 10 ml
Salt to taste	
Red chilli powder to taste	

Serves: **4-6**

Kalmi Bare

Fried mixed gram cakes

INGREDIENTS:

Bengal gram (*chana dal*), soaked for
    4 hours, drained   2 cups / 320 gm
Split black gram (*dhuli urad dal*), soaked
    for 4-5 hours, drained   ½ cup / 75 gm
Salt   1 tsp / 4 gm
Black peppercorns (*sabut kali
    mirch*), freshly ground   12
Ginger (*adrak*), grated   1 tbsp / 24 gm
Green chillies, finely chopped   2-3
Asafoetida (*hing*)   a pinch
Cumin (*jeera*) seeds   1 tbsp / 6 gm
Coriander (*dhaniya*) seeds   2 tbsp / 12 gm
Green coriander (*hara dhaniya*),
    finely chopped   a bunch
Ghee for frying

Serves: **6**

METHOD:

1. Grind the Bengal gram and black gram separately to a coarse and grainy paste. Mix the pastes and the remaining ingredients, except ghee.

2. With wet hands, take some paste and make a 3"-large, round cake. Repeat till all the mixture is used up.

3. Heat the ghee in a pan till hot; deep-fry the cakes, a few at a time. When small bubbles appear on the surface, turn and fry the other side till pale golden. Remove and drain the excess oil on absorbent kitchen towels. Keep aside to cool.

4. Then cut each cake into ¼" slice. Reheat the ghee and fry the slices till golden and crisp. Sprinkle some *chaat* masala and serve with mint chutney (see p. 95).

Green chillies will not split and scatter their
seeds, while being fried, if you prick each chilli
with a fork in 2-3 places before frying it.

Aloo Sabu Dana Bara

Fried potato and sago cakes

INGREDIENTS:

Potatoes, boiled, mashed	500 gm
Sago (*sabu dana*), soaked for 15 minutes, drained	½ cup / 60 gm
Groundnuts (*moongphalli*), coarsely pounded	3⅓ tbsp / 50 gm
Salt to taste	
Ginger (*adrak*), chopped, 1" piece	1
Green chillies, chopped	2-3
Green coriander (*hara dhaniya*), chopped	2½ tbsp / 10 gm
Lemon (*nimbu*) juice	1
Vegetable oil for deep-frying	

METHOD:

1. Mix all the ingredients together except the oil and divide the mixture equally into lemon-sized balls.
2. Heat the oil in a wok (*kadhai*); flatten each ball lightly between the palms and fry, a few at a time, till golden. Remove with a slotted spoon and drain the excess oil on absorbent kitchen towels. Repeat till all the balls are fried.
3. Serve hot with *hare dhaniye ki chutney* (see p. 94).

Serves: **8**

Paneer Pakora

Cottage cheese croquettes

INGREDIENTS:

Cottage cheese (*paneer*), grated	500 gm
Green chillies, chopped	4
Green coriander (*hara dhaniya*), chopped	1 tbsp / 4 gm
White pepper (*safed mirch*) powder	1 tsp / 2 gm
Red chilli powder	1 tsp / 2 gm
Carom (*ajwain*) seeds	½ tsp / ¾ gm
Egg (optional)	1
Garam masala	1 tsp / 2 gm
Gram flour (*besan*)	¾ cup / 75 gm
Vegetable oil for frying	

METHOD:

1. Mix all the ingredients (except gram flour and oil) in a bowl. Now, add the gram flour and mix for 2 minutes into a smooth paste.
2. Heat the oil in a wok (*kadhai*); shape the mixture into balls and slide them in carefully. Fry till the cottage cheese balls are golden brown and crisp. Remove with a slotted spoon and drain the excess oil on absorbent kitchen towels.
3. Serve hot with mint chutney (see p. 95).

Serves: **4**

Ginger can be stored for a longer
times if kept in the bottom shelf
of the refrigerator.

Aloo Kabli

Potato and chick pea delight

INGREDIENTS:

Potatoes, boiled, peeled, diced	300 gm
Chick peas (*kabuli chana*), soaked overnight	1 cup / 150 gm
Mango powder (*amchur*)	1 tsp / 2 gm
Cumin (*jeera*) powder	1 tsp / 1½ gm
Coriander (*dhaniya*) powder	2 tsp / 3 gm
Black salt (*kala namak*)	1 tsp / 4 gm
Red chilli powder	½ tsp / 1 gm
Lemon (*nimbu*) juice	½ tsp / 2½ ml
Salt to taste	

For the garnish:

Ginger (*adrak*), julienned	1 tbsp / 24 gm
Green chillies, finely sliced	1 tbsp
Lemon, cut into wedges	

METHOD:

1. Drain the chick peas and pressure cook with 2 cups of water for about 10 minutes or till soft. Drain and keep aside.
2. Mix all the ingredients thoroughly in a bowl.
3. Serve cold garnished with ginger, green chillies, and lemon wedges.

Serves: **2-4**

Aloo Rolls

Flour breads rolled with potato filling

METHOD:

1. Knead the flour with enough water to make a medium-soft dough. Keep aside.
2. Heat the oil in a pan; add cumin seeds. When it starts crackling, add ginger and green chillies. Mix well. Add potatoes and the remaining spices; mix well. Remove and keep side.
3. Divide the dough equally into 10 portions. Roll each out into a round roti; roast and shallow fry each roti with oil. Repeat till all the rotis are made.
4. Spread 3 tbsp of potato stuffing on each roti and roll tightly. Serve hot.

INGREDIENTS:

Potatoes, boiled, mashed	500 gm
Refined flour (maida)	2½ cups / 250 gm
Vegetable oil	2 tsp / 10 ml
Cumin (jeera) seeds	½ tsp / 1 gm
Ginger (adrak), finely chopped	1"
Green chillies, finely chopped	a few
Turmeric (haldi) powder	½ tsp / 1 gm
Red chilli powder to taste	
Salt to taste	
Vegetable oil for deep-frying	

Serves: **5-6**

Surati Patties

Potato cakes filled with dry
fruits and coconut

INGREDIENTS:

Potatoes, boiled, mashed	500 gm
Salt to taste	
Refined flour (*maida*)	2 tbsp / 20 gm
For the filling, mix well together:	
Coconut (*nariyal*),	
fresh, grated	1 cup / 100 gm
Green coriander (*hara dhaniya*),	
finely chopped	2 cups / 50 gm
Green chillies, finely chopped	2
Garlic (*lasan*), chopped	
(optional)	2 tsp / 6 gm
Cashew nuts (*kaju*), chopped	1 tbsp / 15 gm
Raisins (*kishmish*)	1 tbsp / 10 gm
Sugar	1 tbsp / 20 gm
Salt to taste	
Vegetable oil for deep-frying	

Serves: **6-8**

METHOD:

1. Add salt and flour to the potatoes. Knead into a soft dough.
2. Grease your palms, take a small amount of the potato mixture and shape into a flat, round cake.
3. **For the filling**, mix all the ingredients together except the oil.
4. Put about 2 tsp of the filling in the centre of the cake, roll into a round ball, ensuring that the filling stays in. Flatten into a round cake. Similarly, prepare the other cakes.
5. Deep-fry the cakes on high heat in hot oil till golden brown. Remove and drain the excess oil on absorbent kitchen towels.
6. Serve hot.

To remove the strong smell of
garlic from fingers and knives, rub
them with lemon peel.

Chaat Papri

Flour crispies topped with yoghurt

INGREDIENTS:

Refined flour (*maida*)	1 cup / 100 gm
Semolina (*suji*)	1 tbsp / 10 gm
Salt	½ tbsp
Baking powder	a pinch
Vegetable oil	¾ cup / 150 ml
Vegetable oil for frying	

To serve:

Potatoes, boiled, cubed	½ cup
Chick peas (*kabuli chana*), boiled	½ cup
Tamarind (*imli*) chutney (see p. 7)	¾ cup / 150 gm
Mint chutney (see p. 95)	4 tbsp / 60 gm
Yoghurt (*dahi*), beaten	1 cup / 200 gm
Chaat masala to taste	

Serves: **4**

METHOD:

1. Sift the first four ingredients together. Add hot oil and mix well. Knead with enough water to make a smooth dough.
2. Divide the dough equally

into tiny balls. Roll each out into a very thin disc, 1½" diameter. Perforate each with a fork so that it does not puff out while frying. Keep aside for 30 minutes, uncovered.

3. Deep-fry the discs on medium heat in hot oil till crisp and golden. Remove and drain the excess oil on absorbent paper towels.

4. To serve, arrange the fried discs on a plate; spread the potatoes, chick peas, tamarind and mint chutneys, yoghurt, and *chaat* masala to taste.

Arvi Ki Chaat

Tangy colocasia

INGREDIENTS:

Colocasia (*arvi*), boiled, cubed	500 gm
Salt	2 tsp / 8 gm
Tomatoes, chopped	100 gm
Lemon (*nimbu*) juice	3 tbsp / 45 ml
Green chillies, chopped	4
Green coriander (*hara dhaniya*), chopped	¼ cup / 6 gm
Mint (*pudina*) leaves, chopped	a few
Mango powder (*amchur*)	2 tsp / 4 gm

Serves: **4-6**

METHOD:

1. Combine the salt, tomatoes, lemon juice, green chillies, green coriander, and mint leaves in a bowl. Add the colocasia and mix well.
2. Sprinkle mango powder over the colocasia mixture and serve.

Do not put green tomatoes in the sun to ripen, as they turn soft. Instead, put them in a brown bag and leave it in the sun for three to four days to ripen. They stay firm this way.

Doodh Ka Bhutta

Corn cooked in milk

METHOD:

1. Mix the crushed corn with milk and bring to the boil. Cook, stirring constantly, till the mixture thickens.
2. Add the remaining ingredients; mix well. Remove from heat and serve as a topping on toast or as a stuffing in grilled sandwiches.

INGREDIENTS:

Corn (*bhutta*) kernels, crushed	250 gm
Milk	1¼ cups / 250 ml
Butter	1½ tbsp / 30 gm
Salt	½ tsp / 2 gm
White pepper (*safed mirch*) powder	¼ tsp

Serves: **6**

Milk turned sour can be used to make excellent scones. You can also use it in curries which need a sour flavour, instead of yoghurt.

Suhali

Crisp, fried flour savouries

INGREDIENTS:

Refined flour (*maida*)	2½ cups / 250 gm
Ghee	3 tbsp / 45 gm
Carom (*ajwain*) seeds	tsp / ¾ gm
Salt	½ tsp / 2 gm
Vegetable oil for deep-frying	

METHOD:

1. Mix all the ingredients together except the oil and knead into a stiff dough.
2. Divide the dough equally into 20-25 portions. Roll each portion out into a flat disc of 2" diameter. Pierce each with a fork.
3. Heat the oil in a wok (*kadhai*); fry the discs, a few at a time, on low heat till brown. Remove with a slotted spoon and drain the excess oil on absorbent kitchen towels. Repeat till all the discs are fried.
4. These can be stored for a week in airtight containers and eaten with any pickle of your choice.

Makes: **20-25**

Khandvi

Gram flour rolls

INGREDIENTS:

Gram flour (besan)	2½ cups / 250 gm
Green chillies	4
Ginger (adrak), 1" piece	1
Buttermilk (chaas)	2 cups / 400 ml
Water	2 cups / 500 ml
Turmeric (haldi) powder	½ tsp / 1 gm
Salt to taste	

For the tempering:

Vegetable oil	1 tbsp / 15 ml
Mustard seeds (rai)	1 tsp / 3 gm
Dry red chillies (sookhi lal mirch), cut	2
Asafoetida (hing)	a pinch
Curry leaves (kari patta)	7-8
Coconut (nariyal), grated	¼
Green coriander (hara dhaniya), chopped	1 cup / 25 gm
Green chillies, slit	5

Serves: **6**

METHOD:

1. Grind the green chillies and ginger with a little water to a smooth paste.
2. Mix the buttermilk, gram flour, and water together. Add turmeric powder, salt, and chilli-ginger paste. Mix to make a smooth batter.
3. Cook the batter in a pan on medium heat till a thick paste-like consistency is obtained. Remove.
4. Grease the reverse side of 2 stainless steel flat plates and spread the mixture as thinly as possible.
5. While it is still warm, make 1" wide strips with a sharp knife on the spread mixture. When cool, gently roll each strip to resemble small swiss rolls. Arrange the rolls on a serving platter.
6. **For the tempering,** heat the oil in a pan; sauté

the mustard seeds till it starts spluttering. Add dry red chillies and asafoetida. Sauté for a few seconds, remove from heat and pour over the prepared rolls.

7. Garnish with coconut and green coriander; serve either hot or cold.

Khaman Dhokla

Steamed Bengal gram squares

INGREDIENTS:

Bengal gram (*chana dal*), soaked overnight	1 cup / 160 gm
Green chillies	4
Ginger (*adrak*), 1" piece	1
Vegetable oil	3 tbsp / 45 ml
Salt to taste	
Asafoetida (*hing*)	¼ tsp / 1 gm
Bicarbonate of soda	¼ tsp

For the tempering:

Vegetable oil	1 tbsp / 15 ml
Mustard seeds (*rai*)	½ tsp / 1½ gm
Cumin (*jeera*) seeds	½ tsp / 1 gm
Dry red chillies (*sookhi lal mirch*), whole	3-4
Curry leaves (*kari patta*)	10
Green coriander (*hara dhaniya*), chopped	½ cup / 12½ gm
Coconut (*nariyal*), grated	¼

Serves: **6**

METHOD:

1. Grind the green chillies and ginger to a smooth paste. Keep aside.
2. Grind the Bengal gram coarsely; whisk to incorporate air in it. Keep aside to ferment in a

warm place for at least 10 hours or till tiny bubbles appear. Add the remaining ingredients, chilli-ginger paste, and a little water; whisk the mixture thoroughly

3. Grease a flat steel plate (2" deep). Spread the mixture to a thickness of 1". Steam till it is done. Cool and cut into 1" squares.

4. **For the tempering**, heat the oil in a pan; add the mustard seeds, cumin seeds, and dry red chillies. When they start crackling, add curry leaves and pour over the steamed squares.

5. Serve garnished with green coriander and coconut.

Namak Para

Diamond-shaped flour savouries

INGREDIENTS:

Refined flour (*maida*)	2½ cups / 250 gm
Ghee	3 tbsp / 45 gm
Onion seeds (*kalonji*)	½ tsp / 1 gm
Salt	½ tsp / 2 gm
Vegetable oil for deep-frying	

Serves: **20-25**

METHOD:

1. Mix all the ingredients together except the oil and knead. Roll the dough to a ¼"-thick disc.
2. With a sharp knife cut the disc into ½" wide vertical strips.
3. Again cut in a slant about ½"-wide strips to get diamond shapes.
4. Heat the oil in wok (*kadhai*); fry these pieces, a few at a time, on low heat till brown and crisp. Remove with a slotted spoon and drain the excess oil on absorbent paper towels. Repeat till all the pieces are fried.
5. This can be stored for a week in airtight containers. Serve with any pickle of your choice.

Toor Dal Bara

Deep-fried red gram dumplings

METHOD:

1. Drain the split red gram and blend to a fine paste with the fenugreek seeds. Mix in bicarbonate of soda, salt, and green chillies.
2. Heat the oil in a wok (*kadhai*); drop spoonfuls of this thick batter and fry until uniformly brown and cooked. Remove with a slotted spoon and drain the excess oil on absorbent kitchen towels.
3. Serve hot or cold with any pickle or chutney of your choice.

Note: *The dumplings may be baked in greased cup cake trays in an oven set at 180°C / 350°F for 30-40 minutes.*

INGREDIENTS:

Split red gram (*arhar dal*), soaked in cold water overnight	2 cups / 300 gm
Fenugreek seeds (*methi dana*)	½ tsp / 1½ gm
Bicarbonate of soda	½ tsp
Salt to taste	
Green chillies, finely chopped	2
Vegetable oil for deep-frying	

Serves: **4-6**

Kobi Na Moothia

Steamed cabbage dumplings

INGREDIENTS:

Cabbage (*bandh gobi*), finely shredded	250 gm
Salt to taste	
Gram flour (*besan*)	1 cup / 100 gm
Asafoetida (*hing*)	¼ tsp / 1 gm
Green chillies	3
Ginger (*adrak*) paste	1 tsp / 6 gm
Bicarbonate of soda	¼ tsp
Juice of lemon (*nimbu*)	1
Sugar	1 tbsp / 20 gm
Vegetable oil	2 tbsp / 30 ml
For the tempering:	
Vegetable oil	1 tbsp / 15 ml
Mustard seeds (*rai*)	½ tsp / 1½ gm
Cumin (*jeera*) seeds	½ tsp / 1 gm
Red chilli powder	1 tsp / 2 gm
Curry leaves (*kari patta*)	10
Turmeric (*haldi*) powder	½ tsp / 1 gm
Asafoetida	a pinch

METHOD:

1. Mix the salt with the cabbage; keep aside for 20 minutes. Squeeze out the juice from the cabbage.
2. Add gram flour, and the other ingredients. Knead with enough water to make a soft dough.
3. With wet palms, make sausage-shape rolls; about ½-¾" diameter. Steam the rolls for 15-20 minutes in a steamer. Remove, cool and cut into ½" pieces.
4. **For the tempering,** heat the oil; add the mustard seeds; sauté. Add the remaining ingredients and the steamed rolls; sauté for 5 minutes and serve.

Serves: **4-6**

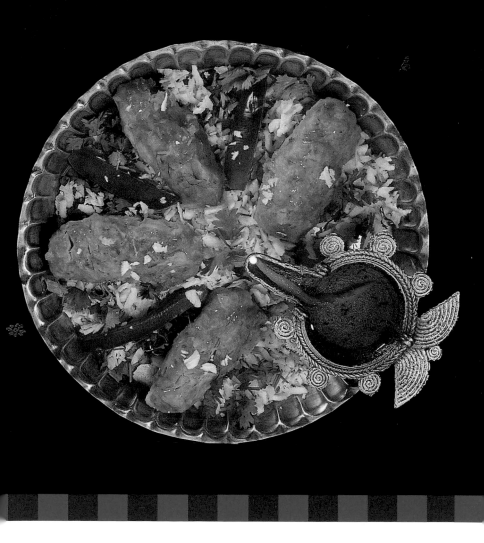

To prevent boiled cabbage from
smelling, place half a slice of
bread tied in a muslin in the
water in which it is being boiled.

Phoolaura

Split black gram fritters

INGREDIENTS:

Split black gram (*urad dal*)
  with skin   1¾ cups / 250 gm
Asafoetida (*hing*)   a pinch
Cumin (*jeera*) seed, ground   ½ tsp / 1 gm
Ginger (*adrak*),
  scraped, ground   1 tsp / 6 gm
Green chillies, ground (optional)   2-3
Salt to taste
Mustard (*sarson*) oil for frying

METHOD:

1. Soak the split black gram overnight. Next morning rub between your palms till the skin comes out. Grind to a paste.
2. Add all the ingredients to the paste and mix with wet hands till the mixture is very light and fluffy.
3. Heat the mustard oil till it starts smoking; lower heat and drop a full tsp of the mixture in batches. Fry till brown. Remove with a slotted spoon and drain the excess oil on absorbent kitchen towels.
4. Serve as a snack with tea.

Serves: **2-4**

Fried food which is not served at
once should not be covered as it
loses its crispness

Chura Tareko

Pressed rice savoury

INGREDIENTS:

Beaten rice (*chidwa*)	3 cups / 150 gm
Vegetable oil for frying	
Potatoes, medium-sized, peeled, cut into thin rounds, soaked in water	2
Groundnuts (*moongphalli*), fried	100 gm
Dry red chillies	4-5
Coconut (*nariyal*), cut into thin slices	4 tsp / 8 gm
Green coriander (*hara dhaniya*), strands	2 cups / 50 gm
Salt to taste	
Turmeric (*haldi*) powder	½ tsp / 1 gm
Cumin (*jeera*) seeds, dry roasted, powdered	1 tsp / 2 gm

METHOD:

1. Heat the oil in a pan; fry a little beaten rice first if it puffs up the oil is of the right temperature. Fry the remaining beaten rice and keep aside.
2. In the same oil, fry the following one at a time in the given order, drain and keep aside: the potato rounds till crisp, groundnuts, dry red chillies till they turn light brown, coconut pieces and green coriander.
3. In a large flat dish, mix all the fried items together.
4. Mix together salt, turmeric powder, and cumin powder. With light fingers, mix everything together. When the mixture cools, store in an airtight container.

Serves: 2-4

To keep boiled potatoes white,
add a few drops of vinegar to the
cooking water.

Bharwan Pappad

Vegetable poppadom rolls

INGREDIENTS:

Poppadoms (*pappad*), medium-sized	4
Carrot (*gajar*), medium-sized, chopped	I
Potato, medium-sized, chopped	I
Cauliflower (*phool gobi*), chopped	100 gm
French beans, chopped	6
Tomatoes, chopped	I
Turmeric (*haldi*) powder	½ tsp / I gm
Red chilli powder	½ tsp / I gm
Green coriander (*hara dhaniya*), chopped	I tbsp / 4 gm
Salt to taste	
Vegetable oil for frying	

METHOD:

1. Boil the first four vegetables with a pinch of salt till ¾ done. Drain and keep aside.
2. Fry the tomatoes in 1 tbsp oil. Add the boiled vegetables, turmeric powder, red chilli powder, and green coriander. Mix well. Remove and keep aside to cool. Divide the mixture equally into 4 portions.
3. Take a poppadom and dip it in water (so that it becomes pliable). Put one portion of this mixture along the centre and roll. Press the ends well to seal. Repeat with the other poppadoms.
4. Heat the oil in a wok (*kadhai*); deep-fry the rolls till crisp. Remove immediately and serve hot.

Serves: **4**

Til Paneer Ke Kebab

Cottage cheese kebabs with sesame seeds

METHOD:

1. Mix all the ingredients till gram flour / cornflour with a wooden spoon for 2 minutes.
2. Divide this mixture equally into 20 balls. Compress each ball slightly to get a 4 cm round patty. Refrigerate the patties for 20 minutes.
3. Sprinkle some sesame seeds over the patties and shallow fry on a griddle until crisp and golden. Alternatively, you could lightly coat each patty with beaten egg white, before sprinkling sesame seeds and frying. Serve hot.

INGREDIENTS:

Cottage cheese (*paneer*), finely grated	500 gm
Green cardamom (*choti elaichi*) powder	½ tsp / 1 gm
Garam masala	2 tsp / 4 gm
Green chillies, chopped	2
Green coriander (*hara dhaniya*), chopped	2 tsp / 4 gm
Mace (*javitri*) powder	½ tsp / 1 gm
Onions, finely chopped	½ cup
White pepper (*safed mirch*) powder	1 tsp / 2 gm
Yellow or red chilli powder	1½ tsp
Yoghurt (*dahi*), drained	2 cups
Salt to taste	
Gram flour (*besan*) / Cornflour	¼ cup / 25 gm
Sesame (*til*) seeds	½ cup / 60 gm
Egg white (optional)	1
Vegetable oil for shallow-frying	

Serves: **6**

89

Aloo Paratha

Potato-stuffed unleavened bread

INGREDIENTS:

Wholewheat flour (*atta*)	½ cup / 50 gm
Ghee	1 tbsp / 15 gm
For the filling:	
Potatoes, boiled, mashed	1 cup
Garam masala	½ tsp / 1 gm
Red chilli powder	¾ tsp / 1½ gm
Coriander (*dhaniya*) seeds, roasted, powdered	1 tsp / 2 gm
Green coriander (*hara dhaniya*), chopped	1 tbsp / 4 gm
Onion, chopped	1 tbsp / 12 gm
Salt to taste	
Ghee for shallow frying	

Serves: **4**

METHOD:

1. Sift the wholewheat flour. Rub in the ghee with your fingertips. Knead with enough cold water to make a soft dough.

2. **For the filling,** mix all the

ingredients together. Divide the filling into 10 equal portions.

3. Divide the dough equally into 10 portions. Flatten each out into a small disc. Place 1 portion of the filling in the centre, press the edges to seal and reshape into a ball. Roll each ball out into an 8"

disc, dusting with dry flour to prevent sticking.

4. Fry the disc on a griddle with 1 tsp ghee, till tiny brown spots appear on both sides. Repeat with the other discs.

5. Serve hot with yoghurt.

Methi Ki Roti

Fenugreek-flavoured unleavened bread

INGREDIENTS:

Wholewheat flour (*atta*)	2 cups / 200 gm
Fenugreek (*methi*) leaves, chopped	1¾ cups / 50 gm
Green coriander (*hara dhaniya*), chopped	1 cup / 25 gm
Green chillies, chopped	2
Salt to taste	
Vegetable oil for shallow frying	

METHOD:

1. Mix the wholewheat flour, fenugreek leaves, green coriander, green chillies, and salt together. Add 1 tbsp oil; knead with enough water to make a smooth dough. Cover and keep aside for 30 minutes.

2. Knead again and divide the dough into lemon-sized balls. Roll each out to a 2" disc, smear some oil on the top surface and fold into a half moon. Fold the half moon again into a triangle. Now roll the triangle out.

3. Heat a griddle (*tawa*); lay a triangle flat on it and cook on both sides till tiny brown spots appear. Drizzle a little oil and fry till golden brown on both sides. Remove and repeat till all are fried.

Serves: **2-3**

Serve *methi ki roti* with
yoghurt, salad, and pickle of
your choice.

Hare Dhaniye Ki Chutney

Green coriander chutney

INGREDIENTS:

Green coriander	
(*hara dhaniya*)	4 cups / 100 gm
Green chillies	2
Ginger (*adrak*), 1" piece	1
Garlic (*lasan*) cloves (optional)	2
Cumin (*jeera*) seeds	½ tsp / 1 gm
Juice of lemon (*nimbu*)	1

Serves: **6-8**

METHOD:

1. Blend all the ingredients except the lemon juice to a smooth paste.
2. Store the relish in a dry glass jar, in the refrigerator.
3. Just before serving, add lemon juice, mix well and serve as an accompaniment.

Note: *If garlic is used then omit cumin seeds.*

Roll lemons on a hard surface and cut them on the cross for maximum juice. Keep them at room temperature before squeezing. You get very little juice if the lemon is taken straight out of the refrigerator.

Pudina Chutney

Mint chutney

INGREDIENTS:

Mint (*pudina*) leaves, chopped	4 cups / 100 gm
Green coriander (*hara dhaniya*), chopped	4 cups / 100 gm
Onions, chopped	2 tbsp / 24 gm
Ginger (*adrak*), chopped	1 tbsp / 24 gm
Green chillies, chopped	4-5
Yoghurt (*dahi*)	½ cup / 100 gm
Mango powder (*amchur*)	1 tsp / 2 gm
Sugar	1 tbsp / 20 gm
Salt to taste	
Black salt (*kala namak*)	1 tsp / 4 gm

Serves: **4**

METHOD:

1. Blend the mint leaves, green coriander, onions, ginger, and green chillies to a smooth paste. Keep aside.
2. In a mixing bowl, whisk yoghurt with mango powder, sugar, salt, and black salt. Add the mint paste and mix well.
3. Serve as an accompaniment.

If you add no water while grinding ginger and garlic and sprinkle it with a bit of salt instead, it will keep for a week in a covered jar even without a refrigerator.

Index